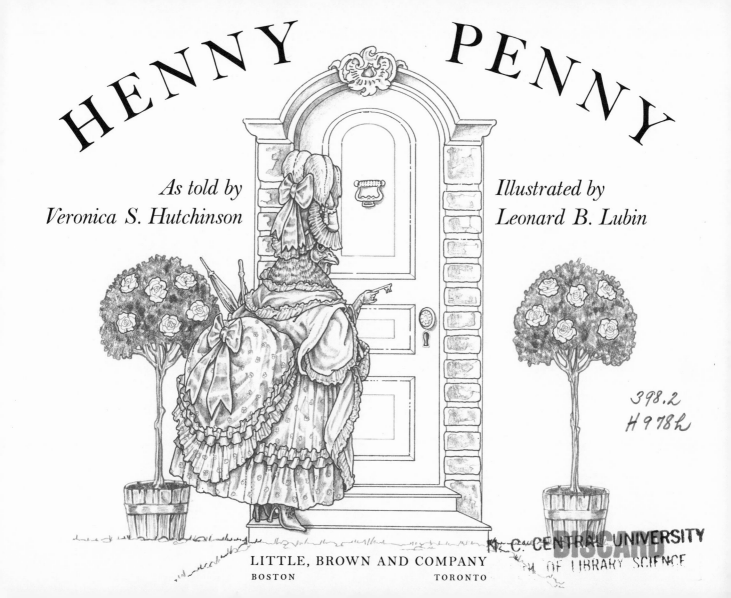

HENNY PENNY

As told by
Veronica S. Hutchinson

Illustrated by
Leonard B. Lubin

LITTLE, BROWN AND COMPANY
BOSTON   TORONTO

Books Illustrated by Leonard B. Lubin

THE PIG-TALE by Lewis Carroll

HENNY PENNY as told by Veronica S. Hutchinson

FIRST EDITION

T 02–76

Text reprinted by permission of G. P. Putnam's Sons from *Chimney Corner Stories* by Veronica S. Hutchinson. Copyright © 1925 Minton, Balch & Co.

In this edition one slight alteration has been made in Veronica Hutchinson's original text.

Library of Congress Cataloging in Publication Data

Hutchinson, Veronica Somerville.
  Henny Penny.

  SUMMARY: Henny Penny and her friends are on their way to tell the king that the sky is falling when they are outwitted by the fox.
  [1. Folklore] I. Lubin, Leonard B. II. Chicken Little. III. Title.
PZ8.1.H973He   [398.2] [E]   75-25647
ISBN 0-316-38400-3

Published simultaneously in Canada
by Little, Brown & Company (Canada) Limited

PRINTED IN THE UNITED STATES OF AMERICA

For my mother

—L. L.

One day Henny Penny was picking up corn in the farm-yard, when an acorn fell out of a tree and struck her on the head.

"Goodness gracious me!" said Henny Penny, "the sky is falling. I must go and tell the King."

So she went along and she went along and she went along until she met Cocky Locky.

"Where are you going, Henny Penny?" asked Cocky Locky.

"Oh," said Henny Penny, "the sky is falling and I am going to tell the King."

"May I go with you, Henny Penny?" asked Cocky Locky.

"Certainly," said Henny Penny.

So Henny Penny and Cocky Locky went to tell the King that the sky was falling.

They went along and they went along and they went along, until they met Ducky Daddles.

"Where are you going, Henny Penny and Cocky Locky?" asked Ducky Daddles.

"Oh, we are going to tell the King that the sky is falling," said Henny Penny and Cocky Locky.

"May I go with you?" asked Ducky Daddles.

"Certainly," said Henny Penny and Cocky Locky.

So Henny Penny, Cocky Locky, and Ducky Daddles
went to tell the King that the sky was falling.

They went along and they went along and they went along until they met Goosey Poosey.

"Where are you going, Henny Penny, Cocky Locky, and Ducky Daddles?" asked Goosey Poosey.

"Oh, we are going to tell the King the sky is falling," said Henny Penny, Cocky Locky, and Ducky Daddles.

"May I go with you?" asked Goosey Poosey.

"Certainly," said Henny Penny, Cocky Locky, and Ducky Daddles.

So Henny Penny, Cocky Locky, Ducky Daddles and Goosey Poosey went to tell the King that the sky was falling.

They went along and they went along and they went along until they met Turkey Lurkey.

"Where are you going, Henny Penny, Cocky Locky, Ducky Daddles, and Goosey Poosey?" asked Turkey Lurkey.

"Oh, we are going to tell the King the sky is falling," said Henny Penny, Cocky Locky, Ducky Daddles, and Goosey Poosey.

"May I go with you?" asked Turkey Lurkey.

"Certainly," said Henny Penny, Cocky Locky, Ducky Daddles, and Goosey Poosey.

So Henny Penny, Cocky Locky, Ducky Daddles, Goosey Poosey, and Turkey Lurkey went on to tell the King the sky was falling.

They went along and they went along and they went along until they met Foxy Woxy.

"Where are you going, Henny Penny, Cocky Locky, Ducky Daddles, Goosey Poosey, and Turkey Lurkey?" asked Foxy Woxy.

"Oh, we are going to tell the King the sky is falling," said Henny Penny, Cocky Locky, Ducky Daddles, Goosey Poosey, and Turkey Lurkey.

"Oh, but that is not the way to the King, Henny Penny, Cocky Locky, Ducky Daddles, Goosey Poosey, and Turkey Lurkey," said Foxy Woxy, "come with me and I will show you a short way to the King's Palace."

"Certainly," said Henny Penny, Cocky Locky, Ducky Daddles, Goosey Poosey, and Turkey Lurkey.

To·Ye·Palace

Ye·ShorT·CuT

They went along and they went along and they went along until they reached Foxy Woxy's Cave. In they went,

and they never came out again.

To this day the King has never been told that the sky was falling.

THE END